I0149513

GOD THOUGHTS

How to Recognize and Respond to the Voice of God

Mildred Simmons

HIGH BRIDGE BOOKS

HOUSTON

God Thoughts: How to Recognize and Respond to the Voice of God
by Mildred Simmons

Copyright © 2014 by Mildred Simmons
All rights reserved.

Printed in the United States of America
Paperback ISBN: 978-1-940024-32-5
eBook ISBN: 978-1-940024-33-2

All rights reserved by the author. The author guarantees all contents are original and do not infringe upon the legal rights of any other person or work. No part of this book may be reproduced in any form without the permission of the author except in the case of brief quotations embodied in critical articles and reviews. If you would like to reproduce this book in any form, please seek permission first by contacting the publisher via www.HighBridgeBooks.com.

Unless otherwise indicated, Bible quotations are taken from *The New American Standard Version— Updated Edition*. NASB. Copyright © 2000 by Zondervan.

www.MildredSimmons.com

ABOUT THE AUTHOR

Mildred Simmons' experience spans over 39 years of bringing people to Jesus Christ with her husband, Jerry, a retired pastor from the United Methodist Church.

Her greatest gift to the Church (reaching across all denominations) is teaching God's Word. She has taught children and adult Sunday Schools, church and home Bible studies, seminars, and has ministered to women from the adult entertainment industry. Mildred's ability to help people understand Biblical truths has brought them to a deeper relationship with God and has enabled many to find their own ministry.

Mildred and Jerry reside in Canyon Lake, Texas and have been married for more than 50 years.

For more information about Mildred, visit **www.MildredSimmons.com** or e-mail her at info@MildredSimmons.com.

CONTENTS

CHAPTER 1

WHAT ARE *GOD THOUGHTS*?

Every day, thousands of thoughts pass through the human mind. Some of these are good thoughts, and some are not. *God Thoughts* is a book about how to recognize, take ownership for, and act on the good thoughts that God has for you.

What are God thoughts? God thoughts are His communication with you. They are His answers to your prayers. They are His counsel. Many times, they are directives that move you to act according to His purposes.

CONVERSATIONS WITH GOD

There was a time in Biblical history when God spoke His thoughts face-to-face with Adam and Eve. They began their lives with God thoughts. They were not sub-intelligent to God but brilliantly intelligent, well-able to communicate with God Almighty on the highest level of thought.

Try to imagine what it must have been like to converse with the Creator of the universe. Adam's and Eve's communication with God during this pristine period of time before sin entered the world is quite interesting. We have not been given much insight into this because there are only a few conversations on record, plus a few that are implied conversations.

Adam named all the animals God created, and he then had a conversation with God in which he spoke of his delight with the creation of Eve.

Conversation had been exchanged between God, Adam, and Eve based on Eve's statement to the serpent about what "God has said."[1]

Then, Adam and Eve had a conversation with God in which they were using blame as a defense for their sin.[2]

Based on these accounts, presumably recorded by Moses, there is Biblical fact to support that Adam and Eve communicated with God by intelligent speech and that God communicated His thoughts back to them with speech.

SEPARATION FROM GOD

It is also a Biblical fact that they dishonored God by disobeying one of His commands. The consequence of their sin caused their spirits to die, losing God's spirit life.[3] The phrase that God used, "you shall surely die," can be translated with the words, "in dying, you shall die." The phrase, "in dying," refers to the spiritual death of the spirit while "you shall die" refers to the natural death of the body.[4] Sin severed their spirits from the spiritual life flow God provided for them, and it shut off Spirit-to-their-spirit communication. God was caused to deal externally with Adam and Eve and all humankind thereafter—not internally, Spirit-to-spirit. The sinful state of humankind put God "outside," so to speak, until God was able to come "inside" a man and a woman by the new birth as offered in the New Covenant. Eventually, God's contact with humankind would become almost nil due to people turning away from Him.

Adam's third son, Seth, was the exception. Seth and his generations wanted to hear from God and keep His ways.

Toward the end, before God destroyed the world with a flood, the godly generations of Seth were reduced to one family who God considered "blameless in his time." That family included Noah, his three sons, and their wives. At the time of Noah's generation, people became so corrupt with evil and so void of the influence of God's Word that "God regretted He had made man on the earth."[5] God sent a flood to destroy all life on earth, but He brought Noah and his family safely through the flood.[6]

From Noah came his son, Shem, and from Shem's lineage came the generation with the family that gave birth to Jesus Christ, God's very own Son.

Because of God's redemption through Jesus' sacrifice, sin was remitted, and all humankind was freed from sin's death penalty.[7] Through Jesus' resurrection to life, humankind can be "born again" into that new life.[8]

By accepting Jesus' sacrifice for your sins, you are born again of God's Spirit and have access to God thoughts in your re-created spirit. Your re-created spirit is created in righteousness that makes it a habitation wherein God's presence can dwell by His

Holy Spirit.

This plan has been God's desire since "before the world began."[9] How does He make this plan known to us? It comes to "light through the gospel"[10] that men and women are appointed to proclaim.

I have greatly simplified the story of God's plan for saving the world He so loved. God's New Covenant brings us good news that you can receive, allowing you to recognize God thoughts from His Spirit to your spirit again. God has provided an easy exchange of thoughts so that you may hear from Him every day of your life.

Because sin's influence is still in the world today,[11] how can you know for sure that a thought is truly from God? The answer to that bothersome question brings me to the purpose of this book.

In *God Thoughts*, you will find point-by-point information on how to recognize God's thoughts. By recognizing them, you can understand that these thoughts belong to you. Taking ownership of them will lead you to do whatever is necessary to see that God's purpose is realized.

The reflection questions and "Power Points" following each chapter will build up your confidence for taking action on these thoughts.

Also, the *God Thoughts Journal*, which is located at the end of this book, is a unique method for developing a "hearing ear." Using these tools, you can become renewed to gain a fresh perspective about God thoughts, and you can learn how to achieve the results God desires for you.

Clearly, I am not referring to the hearing that comes through the two ears located on the left and right sides of your head. I am referring to the hearing of these thoughts on the inside of you: your inner-self, your spirit.[12] By His Spirit, God communicates with your spirit. This is where your hearing becomes finely tuned to God's voice. Developing confidence in hearing with your spirit's ear is essential for recognizing, taking ownership for, and acting on God thoughts.

Through the enabling by God, developing that kind of hearing is within your ability. If it were not so, Jesus would not have said this: "...the sheep know his voice: and he calls his own sheep by name..." Jesus named Himself "the Good Shepherd," and said that you, his "sheep," will know his voice and not the voice of a stranger.[13] The Good Shepherd knows your name, and He knows your thoughts, every one of them.

Knowing your thoughts is not unusual for Jesus. Even while on earth, He knew the thoughts of men. The Bible says, "Jesus, knowing their thoughts said..."[14] As He is now sitting on the throne with God the Father,[15] Jesus continues to know our thoughts.

We have references that King David knew this about God as well. He said, "Thou knowest my down-sitting and mine uprising, thou understandest my thought afar off...thou art acquainted with all my ways."[16] David also said, "The LORD knows the thoughts of man..."[17]

The ability to know and receive God thoughts is part of being made in God's image and in His likeness.[18] You are a spirit with a soul that lives in a body. Your spirit has to be made alive again with the life of God. God does not use your old spirit for this. When you became born again, He created a new spirit for you. The literal Greek translation means "a new creature," which implies that this *creature* never before existed.[19] Also, this verse explains that the "old" was done away with and that all things are "new."

There is a bonus for you as well that helps with identifying God thoughts. You now have the "mind of Christ."[20]

These scriptures strongly substantiate evidence that you can rely on your spirit to receive the thoughts of God.

REFLECTION

Every one of us needs reinforcements at one time or another. Making the greatest impact with your God thoughts is built into this workshop. Completing the questions will help to bring positive thought patterns into focus and will help to address the damage that comes with doubt, indecision, and discouragement.

It is the word of power from God that renews your mind to His way of thinking. Being renewed to God's way of thinking makes it easy for recognition of God thoughts. That is why Hebrews 1:3 plays a major role in reinforcing what you have read. Jesus "upholds all things by the word of His power." That is exciting, knowing you can receive His thoughts for your life and help others. You can expect the upholding word of His power to produce results.

What is a "God Thought"?

Who were the original people in the Bible who received God thoughts?

How did humankind lose the ability to receive God thoughts, and how was this ability regained?

How can you know for sure that a thought is truly from God?

What is the "hearing ear" as defined by the author?

Developing the hearing ear builds up what for you?

How do you know this ear can be developed and finely tuned to God's voice?

Our ability to receive and know God thoughts is ascribed to what? Give supporting scriptures.

Write the "Bonus" scripture.

POWER POINTS

"For you have been born again not of seed which is perishable but imperishable, that is, through the living and abiding word of God." (1 Peter 1:23)

"Therefore, if any man is in Christ, he is a new creature; the old things passed away; behold new things have come, now all these things are from God..." (2 Corinthians 5:17-18a)

"We know that we are of God, and the whole world lies in the power of the evil one. And we know that the Son of God has come, and has given us understanding in that we might know Him who is true and we are in Him who is true, in His Son Jesus Christ." (1 John 5:19-20)

"He will guide you into all the truth..." (John 16:13)

[Jesus said] "...the sheep hears his voice, and he calls his own sheep by name,"... "the sheep follow him because they know his voice." (John 10:3-4)

---

[1] Genesis 3:3

[2] Genesis 3:9-13

[3] Genesis 2:17

[4] *Vine's Expository Dictionary of Biblical Words* (Nashville: Thomas Nelson Publishers, 1985), 167.

[5] Genesis 6:6

[6] Genesis 7:17-23; 8:13

[7] Colossians 2:12-14

[8] John 3:5-7

[9] 2 Corinthians 5:17; Matthew 13:35; 25:34

[10] 2 Timothy 1:9-11

[11] 1 John 5:19

[12] Ephesians 3:16

[13] John 10:3-4; 14

[14] Matthew 9:4

[15] Hebrews 1:3

[16] Psalms 139:2-3

[17] Psalms 94:11a

[18] Genesis 1:26

[19] 2 Corinthians 5:17; *Vine's Expository Dictionary of Biblical Words*, Thomas Nelson Publishers, 1985, p. 137; from *Notes on Galatians*, by Hogg and Vine, p. 339.

[20] 1 Corinthians 2:16

CHAPTER 2

THERE IS A PROBLEM, THOUGH

Too little experience with a committed prayer time and too little knowledge about God's ways produce a compound problem: no clear recognition of God thoughts. As a result, there is no ownership of them and that means no action on them. When you own a thing, you use it for its advantages. Even if the thing is new, you learn how to use it.

During my 35 years in ministry with my pastor and husband, Jerry, I have found that this problem is all too common among God's people. The frustration that comes from uncertainty about the question, "Is this God or not?", is a tug-of-war for the newly converted and the seasoned Christian alike. Their uncertainty causes them to miss being used by God in blessing others (that includes ministering in the spiritual gifts), and they miss His plans and opportunities for their own lives as well.

I will be honest with you. It was a problem for me, too, so I became committed to developing my spiritual ear for hearing God thoughts. I do not have a perfect record of hearing God, but my record for listening and obeying has improved greatly because of my commitment.

Expressing thoughts to God is something Christians do all the time. I do not know a Christian who has difficulty praying to God concerning their needs and desires. Yet prayer is two-directional: upward and downward.

Prayer to God goes "up." You expect God's ear to be open and ready for your prayers.

Thoughts from God (His answers) come "down." I believe it is fair to say that God expects your ear to be open and ready for His thoughts. Unfortunately, it is the downward direction (hearing God) where problems arise. This is because we neglect two practices: listening to God and learning about God. Our knowledge about God should always be increasing. Neglecting these two practices gives the devil advantages in your life.

The devil would like nothing better than to render you an ineffective Christian. Jesus describes an ineffective person as "salt that is no longer savory, but worthless, thrown out and trampled underfoot by men."[1] God cannot use "non-salty," ineffective men and women for His purposes any more than you can use non-savory salt to flavor your food. One who is like "non-savory salt" cannot accomplish the will of God in the earth, and that is tragic.

Your continued practice of listening for God thoughts and increasing your knowledge about God will keep you "salty," ready to be at His service when the time comes. Jesus said that you are the "salt of the earth."[2] Think about that, especially in light of what Jesus taught us to pray: "Thy kingdom come, Thy will be done on earth as it is in heaven."[3]

God thoughts are God's words sent by His Spirit to your spirit. They are sent to you, personally. They belong to you, and He intends for you to take ownership of them.

These thoughts are words of His power. Hebrews 1:3 explains that God is upholding all things by the word of His power. God thoughts bring His words that are filled with power to uphold you in every situation of life. Imagine the marvelous benefits for you and for the Church if all of His thoughts become realized. The effects would create great testimonies that would grab even the world's attention. With hope, the world would run to the Church for answers to their problems instead of running around in endless circles of futility. All would see the empowerment (being *blessed* means "an empowerment to prosper") that comes when the messages of God thoughts are delivered.

REFLECTION

Describe briefly the "compound problem" and the reason for it.

Give two results that happen when we do not take ownership of our own God thoughts.

The author states that prayer has two directions. What are they?

What direction of prayer gives rise to problems?

What is the reason for the problems?

What does Satan delight in doing to Christians according to the author?

What did Jesus say we are in the earth?

When does this condition become tragic?

POWER POINTS

God expects us to establish His will in the earth. Jesus gave instruction for us to pray, and he believes we will do it. "Thy Kingdom come, Thy will be done on earth as it is in heaven." (Matthew 6:10, KJV)

---

[1] Matthew 5:13
[2] Ibid.
[3] Matthew 6:10, KJV

CHAPTER 3

TWO MAJOR ENEMIES

The lack of discernment caused by too little experience in prayer, too little listening for God thoughts, and too little knowledge about God gives rise to two major enemies of the Christian: doubt and indecision. Doubt and indecision are two of Satan's best buddies. I estimate that these two enemies are responsible for 99 percent of missed and, often times, dismissed God thoughts.

Doubt and indecision are used by Satan for running interference with God's plans for you. In a football game, the quarterback wants to pass the football to his receiver. The receiver encounters defensive moves that interfere with his ability to catch the pass. There are rules that regulate when defensive moves become illegal interference against the receiver. When this happens, everybody usually knows: the fans in the stands, the television viewers, the players, the coaches, and the officials. I say *usually* because there are times when the officials do not know and do not flag it for a penalty. They missed the illegal move, and the guilty player gets away with committing illegal interference against the receiver. This kind of interference presents opportunities for serious injuries.

Satan works in the same way. He does his best to hide under doubt and indecision, hoping to get away with fooling and confusing you about God thoughts. It's illegal, but if he can run interference on you and injure you, he will. When you are dealing with God thoughts and God's written Word, Satan will try to plant doubt and indecision in your thoughts. Satan wants you to miss what God is *passing* to you.

Have you ever received something from God and then questioned, "Is this from

God, or is this from me?" Remember, you have the Word of God for reference. You are the *referee* who has the right to flag a penalty on Satan and make him pay. However, if you do not seek an answer from the correct source, watch out; doubt and indecision have entered the game. They want to defeat you.

You should also beware that you can doubt and still act. Let's look at Eve in the Garden of Eden as her big mistake is happening.[1] The devil entices Eve by throwing doubt around in response to God's command not to eat the fruit from the Tree of the Knowledge of Good and Evil. Doubt is in her presence; it grabs her mind. Instead of stopping at doubt's confusing mix of words from the serpent, Eve continues acting on the serpent's explanation of what God's command *really* means. She is not seeking clarification from God, the right source. Consequently, Eve acts by choosing doubt's deceit, committing sin, and losing everything in life. The Bible says that, by this wrong decision of Adam and Eve (sin of disobedience and not honoring God), death entered the world, and death by sin came to all men, for all men continued to sin after that.[2]

In addition to the devil's clever use of doubt that questions God and yourself, doubt can bring indecision that will shut down your ability to act on God thoughts. Indecision can result in a "prayer jam." I am referring to indecision that can hold you back due to doubt's grip on your thinking. Consequently, there is no moving forward with God on His thoughts. I call this being caught in a "prayer jam." Let me explain.

Let's say you are driving on a two-way street, and you and all other cars are traveling in one direction only. Eventually, you stop at an intersection for a red light. The light turns green. The cars in front of you go their different ways, but you do not make a move. At this point, you cannot make up your mind about what direction you should take. Go forward? Turn left? Turn right? Indecision has you stalled at the intersection, and your indecision is causing a traffic jam. The longer you sit, the more cruel frustration becomes for you, not to mention for the others lined up behind you. You are praying about it, but frustration is taking over. Your "hearing ear" gets clogged with many thoughts because indecision has stopped everything from moving forward with God in that moment. You cannot decide whether you are really hearing from God.

This kind of jam happens to every one of us Christians, so you are not alone in this. As a specific example, I allowed indecision to keep me from obeying a God Thought that turned into an invitation. It was during a seminar I attended when I noticed a Bible verse that kept coming to my mind about money, a verse that would be very suitable for the offering time. I mentioned the scripture to the leader, and she paused momentarily in deep thought. Then, she looked at me with eyes full of penetrating insight and asked if I would like to address the offering that evening. I did not say "yes" or "no," and she wisely advised me to pray about it. I did pray, but I could not decide if I should be the one to address the offering.

When time came for the offering, I was standing in the back of the pavilion, waiting for the "right feeling" to move me. I thought that, surely the leader would call me up, but she did not. She kept talking about the offering and kept looking at me, expecting me to come forward. I prayed, "Lord, doesn't she know I need more than a glance? Why doesn't she only invite me to come verbally? Then, I will know for sure I am supposed to do this." I was waiting for the leader to provide a sign for me.

If I had known then what I know now about examining all of my options, I would not have been stuck in that jam because all the signs were in place. Only, I could not recognize them. I could not recognize that it started with the thought I had. It was confirmed by an invitation from the leader. And I already knew what to say in the address. What more did I expect?

As it turned out, she did not invite me to come up front. She already had extended the invitation and left it up to me to make the next move. I should have walked up, but I did nothing. I blew it. I missed a great opportunity to bless others with understanding through that scripture about giving, which would have blessed the funding of the seminar. Indecision held its grip on me. Consequently, I did not go anywhere with that wonderful God Thought. Thank God He showed me a remedy for these frustrating situations.

REFLECTION

Name the two major enemies of the Christian. What is their origin?

According to the author, what is the estimated percentage of missed and dismissed God thoughts caused by these two enemies?

Describe the point of the example with the quarterback wanting to pass the football to his receiver. Describe your position in this example.

POWER POINTS

You have the "rule book," the Bible, which states your rights and privileges in this life through Christ Jesus. Romans 5:17 says, "For if by the transgression of the one, death reigned through the one, much more those who receive the abundance of grace and of the gift of righteousness will reign in life through the One, Jesus Christ." You reign "like a king" in life by Jesus Christ over all the powers of darkness. Flag and penalize Satan! Kick him out of your game!

What is another thing you should know about doubt?

How did this work with Eve?

God knows our faulty areas, and He still loves us in spite of them. His forgiveness through Christ Jesus is the benefit of a debt that has been paid. Our sins have been remitted.

"And when you were dead in your transgressions and the uncircumcision of your flesh, He made you alive together with Him, having forgiven us all our transgressions." (Colossians 2:13)

"Who is a God like Thee, who pardons iniquity and passes over the rebellious act of the remnant of His possession? He does not retain His anger forever, Because He delights in unchanging love. He will again have compassion on us; He will tread our iniquities under foot. Yes, Thou wilt cast all their sins into the depths of the sea." (Micah 7:18-19)

What is the harm that indecision causes? What is this effect called by the author?

---

[1] Genesis 3:1-6
[2] Romans 5:12

CHAPTER 4

THE WAY OUT OF A PRAYER-JAM

Be cool... Stay cool... The Bible says, "And he who has a cool spirit is a man of understanding."[1] You may think that our generation has a monopoly on the word, *cool*. Ha! God used it first. Thank God that He has not left you alone with your self-effort for getting out of a jam. Now, this is what you do. Cool down the frustration; it is only a distraction. Collect your wits, and make good use of your options at hand. There is no traffic in the lane going the opposite direction. Make a U-turn. Go back to the written Word of God.

The Bible gives the truth about God's nature and His instructions pertaining to life. There are Bibles with study helps, study guides, subject listings, and word concordances. Some Bible editions provide Hebrew and Greek definitions to offer clearer meanings of translated words. Locate scriptures that define God's character, ways, and wisdom. Review the ministry of Jesus. These methods will help you to identify those things that are of the Spirit of God. As you identify the things of God, you will turn away from the things that lead you into error.

Proper instruction leads to proper action. Every inspiration, thought, direction, voice, gut feeling, or hunch should and must agree with His written Word. No exceptions! If the thought agrees with His nature, His ways, His love, and His description of righteousness (ways and things that are right in His sight), keep it. If it does not, reject it. You are in control of what to do with each of your thoughts.

Rejecting thoughts is what the Bible describes as "casting down." You are taking control of those thoughts that do not conform to God by,

...casting down imaginations and every lofty thing that rises up against the knowledge of God, and we are taking every thought captive to the obedience of Christ.[2]

This scripture gives excellent insight into how to manage all thoughts that come to your mind. It is up to you to judge every thought and bring every thought into obedience to Jesus Christ. You will begin to see that most thoughts fall into two categories: negative and positive. You can turn negative to positive by measuring these thoughts against the teachings of Jesus Christ. As you continue seeking Him through His Word, you will find it easier to identify incoming God thoughts.

Not only do U-turns help you to identify true God thoughts, they fortify you as well. For example, on milk cartons, you will find the added vitamins and minerals listed on the side. The milk is fortified, built up, and empowered with vitamins and minerals that provide health for your physical body.

Likewise, U-turns toward God's Word will provide added spiritual strength for your inner man. During these study times, you are gaining more knowledge, fortifying your faith in God, and moving in His ways. Your confidence is being strengthened for taking that first step of faith toward receiving God thoughts.

REFLECTION

List the four steps given for getting out of a prayer-jam.

What is the step that moves you in the correct direction?

What are the two things stated in this section that the Bible gives truth about?

In addition to reviewing Jesus' ministry, what is the main reason why you need to locate scriptures that define God's character, ways, and wisdom for identifying God thoughts?

What should you do with inspirations, thoughts, direction, voices, gut feelings, or hunches?

Name the things with which your thoughts must agree.

What is the act of "casting down" according to 2 Corinthians 10:5?

Using the milk carton comparison example, describe the results of U-turns toward the Bible.

POWER POINTS

"For the word of God is living and active and sharper than any two-edged sword, and piercing as far as the division of soul and spirit, of both joints and marrow, and able to judge the thoughts and intentions of the heart." (Hebrews 4:12)

---

[1] Proverbs 17:27b
[2] 2 Corinthians 10:5

CHAPTER 5

IS THIS FROM GOD OR FROM ME?

Some thoughts are obviously God thoughts. You heard words that were not formed by your mind, and there's no question that these thoughts were interjected into your thinking by God. You still need to judge those thoughts for God's character.

But what about the thoughts that are not so obvious to you? You think they are God thoughts, but you are not sure. Again, judge them in view of God's character. If you are still questioning, "Is it God or me?" do not be afraid to assume the thought came from you. Why? God is using you to hear Him. His Holy Spirit is speaking to your spirit, and your spirit is telling you what He said. There isn't anyone else in there but you! You are hearing from your spirit in you.

God thoughts usually arrive softly and quietly, not with "goose bumps" or some other feeling. They seem so ordinary that you could easily ignore them and throw them away. Do not be hasty when judging quiet thoughts. Examine the content and context first before doing anything with the thought (see section titled "Judging Thoughts"). The thought should always reflect God, His ways, and His law of love. If you come up with a good idea—if it is a thought that blesses—it is from God. The Bible says, "Every good thing bestowed and every perfect gift is from above, coming down from the Father of lights."[1]

I want to tell you a story of the ordinary voice I heard that was a God Thought. I was in a grocery store's checkout line. Ahead of me were two women. One was very young. She was holding a baby, straddled on her hip. I assumed that the other woman was her mother. Very quietly, a thought came to me to ask them if they would accept some clothes because I surmised they both could wear my dress size. The dresses were already marked for donation, and it seemed good to ask them if they wanted the clothes. No special warning came with this thought. No buzz. No bells. In fact, the thought seemed more like a suggestion of my mind than a thought from God.

Doubt began to creep in. Doubt reminded me that these two women and I were strangers to each other, that I might embarrass them, and that I do not have the clothes with me. To get the clothes, they would have to come to my house, and I assumed they would not want to do that. So, I retreated from making the offer and said nothing to them as we advanced through the checkout line.

Just as I was about to abandon the whole idea, the thought came softly again. Why not go on and ask? All they can do is say, "No, thank you." I decided I would ignore doubt's comments and introduce myself to them in a friendly way. After doing that, I asked the question, and they were delighted to receive the clothes.

At my home, I bubbled with more friendly chatter, hoping to make them feel comfortable. They were polite and smiled a few times, but they did not have anything to say. I mentioned Jesus in our conversation and how He blesses people, and I spoke of being glad that they could use the clothes.

Finally, the mother broke into my one-sided conversation and began speaking of her son. She said he recently started attending church and was always reading his Bible. He was also trying to get her to go to church with him. She mentioned a few other details about her son that made me wonder if I might know him. I finished up with the clothes and was saying goodbye when I asked my last question. I asked her, "What is the name of your son?" To my astonishment, I did know him! Her son was Michael (*name changed*), the young man with whom I had become acquainted several months prior.

Let me tell you about Michael. My husband, Jerry, and I met Michael at a Christian coffee house that was supported by different churches in our town. At that time, he was about 17 and had been born again recently. He wanted all of God he could get. He smiled all the time, enjoyed being among other believers, was very friendly and out-going, and was always clutching his Bible. He was also very, very poor. His body was too skinny for his frame. He wore jeans that were many sizes too large for him, which were held up by a rope tied through the jean's belt loops. He went everywhere barefoot because he owned no shoes. He always wore a very worn-out shirt that was missing some buttons.

All who befriended Michael discerned that his home situation was not good. Michael said that His father threw away every Bible Michael received, and his father ordered him to stop praying. He had to hide his Bible and sneak away to go to church.

Despite his grim circumstances, Michael beamed with joy. I never saw him feeling down because of his circumstances. There was one thing Michael desired most, and he prayed continually for it. He wanted his mother to go to church with him. He told us her reason for not going was because she did not have a dress to wear to church.

It was that soft, ordinary God Thought that I almost ignored that gave Michael's mother a dress to wear to church. Looking back on how everything came together for Michael's answer to his prayer, I marveled at how God answered. This was a big lesson learned in discernment that I reflect back on every time I hear a quiet, soft thought trying to get my attention. So, do not worry about hearing yourself; you could be hearing God.

REFLECTION

Have you ever had an obvious God thought? Please give description of your thought.

Why should you not be afraid to assume that a thought came from you?

What did you learn about how God speaks to you?

Describe a soft, ordinary thought in your own words.

What did you gain from reading the story about Michael and his mother?

POWER POINTS

"Every good thing bestowed and every perfect gift is from above, coming down from the Father of lights." (James 1:17)

---

[1] James 1:17

CHAPTER 6

MAKING A MISTAKE

What if you do something in response to what you consider to be a God Thought and later discover it might have been a mistake? Well, I have done that.

Did God fall off of His throne when I messed up? No, He did not. Did He scold me with scriptures or ignore me for a few days? No, He did not. A wise person said God knows what He got when He got you. He knows what He is dealing with, and He will deal with it through the grace of Jesus. Grace came with Jesus,[1] and you cannot use it up; it doesn't run out. This scripture reveals how God deals with your mistakes:

> My son, do not reject the instruction of the LORD, or loathe His reproof. For whom the LORD loves He reproves, even as a father, the son in whom he delights.[2]

Did I "feel" like a "son in whom he delights?" No, I did not immediately, but those words did help me to get out of what came next: guilt and condemnation.

Guilt and condemnation do not come from God but from the devil. I resisted both of those feelings, repented for my mistake, received my forgiveness, and learned from my mistake. God is well able and willing to straighten out our mistakes when we are willing to allow Him to do so. He is bigger than our mistakes.

God is looking for your willingness and availability when He wants something done. When you are willing to make a move, God delights in that part. I think more highly of a person making a move than of a church full of Christians doing nothing.

God will have you sit down awhile so that He can teach you about serving. You will get up, armed with what you have learned, and you will become available to Him again.

    These experiences remind me of when I first learned how to ride a bicycle. Many times, I fell off my bike. My choice was either to get back on it or stay down. Every time, I chose to get back on and keep riding.

REFLECTION

If you make a mistake with your God thought, how should you to reconcile it?

How can you expect God to deal with your mistake?

POWER POINTS

"My Son do not reject the discipline of the LORD, or loathe His reproof, for whom the LORD loves He reproves, even as a father, the son in whom he delights." (Proverbs 3:11-12)

---

[1] John 1:16-17
[2] Proverbs 3:11-12

CHAPTER 7

GIVING CORRECTION AND ADVICE

In following through with God thoughts for helping others, you must give each thought serious consideration for content and action. Be very wary of thoughts that come as correction or advice for someone. That person is responsible for making their own decisions and corrections about their situations. Do not take their responsibility on yourself.

It is simply not love to throw someone's faults and mistakes in their face by approaching them with your correction or advice. You may find that your correction or advice will not register with them, and you can cause them to sink further into defensiveness. There will be times when you will receive God's wisdom for specific problems. These may be thoughts that God wants you to keep before Him in prayer concerning the person and the problem. It will be a time not to speak but to pray for them. Keep seeking God by interceding for them. Your prayer in these cases should be what the Apostle James describes as "the effectual fervent prayer" that "availeth much."[1] You are *availing* the power of God to work in the situation so that awareness of needed correction or advice can be realized by the person.

A few years ago, I found myself in a situation where I had to intercede for a young woman who was eight-months pregnant and a single parent of a two-year-old boy. She had no plans to get married. When I learned the facts of this woman's situation, right away, I had thoughts about advising her. I believe it was good advice because I had asked for God's wisdom. But I had to keep all of it to myself and before God in prayers of intercession.

The young mother, Marcy (*name changed*), was experiencing a great deal of angst and confusion about trying to make an important decision. She had to decide either to keep her baby or to give the baby for adoption, and her final decision had to be made by a set date. Marcy felt she needed spiritual guidance to help her through the emotional turmoil and confusion she was having. I was contacted by her counselor who allowed Marcy and I to discuss privately the things that were bothering Marcy. We discussed her options and her progress made toward making a decision about her baby. At the end of each visit, we prayed together for her and her family.

Although Marcy was a Christian, she struggled with her trust in God. Also, she felt that, as the baby's mother, giving her baby for adoption would be a sin. The pain of condemnation and hurting emotions registered in her face and body language as we talked. My heart went out to her. As much as I wanted to advise her, I knew I could not do that. In each visit, Marcy pressed me for the answer to her decision. She wanted me to make up her mind for her. Obviously, Marcy was evading her responsibility.

When the time drew near for her final decision, she pleaded with me for an answer. At that moment, I recognized this was the right time to speak this one God Thought that I had received. Leaning closely in to her, I caught her eyes, hoping she could see love in my eyes. I said,

> Marcy, God wants you to know that He is well able to care for you and make things work out by your trusting Him if you decide to keep your baby or if you decide to give your baby for adoption. He will provide for you, for your child, and for your baby in whatever you decide. He will work it out for you.

It finally clicked with Marcy that God was with her, not against her. She left our visit with a changed countenance because of the newfound peace that came from hearing that one God Thought. Marcy didn't tell me her decision, and that was our last visit.

As you can understand from Marcy's story, the timing for delivery of that one God Thought was crucial to her making a decision. Knowing the right time to speak comes from intercessory prayer. Thoughts about giving advice and correction should be slathered with prayer coverage, serious prayer coverage, because you do not want to hurt anyone. Sometimes, we are to reveal what we have heard. At other times, we are not to reveal what we have heard. If it is to be revealed, the revelation will always be handled with love as though Jesus Himself is handling the situation with healing words. Jesus never condones wrong decisions on our part, nor does He ever condemn us for them. He brings correction and then gets us over the *wrongs* in our lives as we choose to follow His advice and obey Him.

Sometimes, the devil uses scripture, too. But, he always uses scripture out of context. He will use it either against you or against someone else, or He will use it to entice you to test God. You can outsmart the devil by doing U-turns to the Bible, conscientiously examining each thought for godly content and scriptural context.

Now, let's go deeper for more understanding about the remedy for doubt and indecision.

REFLECTION

From the story about Marcy, the young pregnant woman, tell what finally clicked with her.

Write the author's conclusion about revealing God thoughts of correction and advice.

POWER POINTS

"A talebearer revealeth secrets: but he that is of a faithful spirit concealeth the matter." (Proverbs 11:13, KJV)

"The preparations of the heart in man and the answer of the tongue are from the LORD." (Proverbs 16:1, KJV)

Does Satan use scripture? How? How do you outsmart Satan?

It is extremely important to examine the content and context of every thought.

---

[1] James 5:16

CHAPTER 8

GOD'S TWO-WAY STREET

First, you should understand that God earnestly desires to communicate with you. God thoughts are coming to you on a daily basis. Because you and I are His children, made in His image, we possess the marvelous privilege of choosing words and speaking them. He created us equipped for God-like conversation (on a level with Him) and for fellowship. He longs for that fellowship, the kind of fellowship a loving family enjoys with one another.

Second, I will show you that God has a "two-way street" of communication with you. You use it every time you read the Bible. Although the Bible was written by men, the words they wrote were inspired by God. The Bible says, "All scripture is inspired by God…"[1] Your Heavenly Father speaks primarily to you through His written Word. He can communicate with you by dreams, visions, prophetic gifts, and an audible voice, too. Here, we are focused on how He communicates through His written Word.

As you read His Word, thoughts will begin coming from Him that bring understanding of what you are reading. God knows your need to *see* how everything works. He knows you learn best through illustrations and word pictures that are familiar to you. In the same way that Jesus explained things using familiar circumstances, God explains by sending forth His Word with an illustration that is familiar. This illustration is one you can see in your natural life and understand. This illustration comes from Isaiah 55:8-11. I call this illustration God's "two-way street"— that is, from heaven to earth and from earth to heaven.

For My thoughts are not your thoughts, Neither are your ways My ways, declares the LORD. For as the heavens are higher than the earth, So are My ways higher than your ways, And My thoughts than your thoughts. For as the rain and the snow come down from heaven, and do not return there without watering the earth, And making it bear and sprout, And furnishing seed to the sower and bread to the eater. So shall My word be which goes forth from My mouth; it shall not return to Me empty, without accomplishing what I desire, and without succeeding in the matter for which I sent it.

From these scriptures, we see that rain and snow have characteristics that are unique, and these work according to physical laws that God created. Rain and snow have a *source, energy,* and a *purpose.* The *source* originates from God's creation of the earth. We know that physical laws cause the falling of rain and snow to the earth.

The falling rain and snow are using and expending *energy* that supplies the earth with one of life's essential needs: water. I like the word, *expending,* because it tells what is happening to the energy. *Expending* means that, as something is working, it is being used up. Thus, I can say that the energy of rain and snow is being used up as it is falling to the earth and filling the soil. Energy is also being expended as the soil swells with moisture.

Getting water to the earth's soil is the *purpose* of rain and snow. The water is causing the earth to bear and sprout by mixing with all of the chemical components of the soil so that life can come forth from the seed. After the sprouts come up through the soil and ripen, then comes the harvest. The harvest furnishes more "seed for the sower and bread for the eater." After successfully fulfilling their purpose in the earth, rain and snow vaporize back to the heavens, and that process completes the natural cycle of rain and snow.

HOW GOD'S "TWO-WAY STREET WORKS" FOR YOU

Effective communication between two people is like a two-way street that has traffic flowing in both directions. Good communication, figuratively speaking, should flow in the same manner—that is, in both directions, from speaker to listener and from listener to speaker.

I want you to think of God conversing with you in the same manner. His communication (God thoughts) comes down to us by His Holy Spirit to our spirit. Some people mistakenly think they need to "pray up a sweat" before God will speak with them. That idea is far from the truth. This is what I believe God is saying about receiving His word:

> See how easily the snow and rain fall? I send My thoughts to you in the same easy manner (by His created spiritual laws that work in heaven and in earth). Therefore, My thoughts to you involve no struggle on your part. Listen for their arrival. My thoughts are full of My love and purpose, falling down to you. Receive them, learn and obey that they may return to Me completed.

In this illustration from Isaiah 55, God uses a *natural law* to explain a *supernatural, spiritual law*, showing you the spiritual cycle of His thoughts coming to you. He shows that the *source, energy,* and *purpose* of the rain and snow are the same for His Word coming down to the earth.

You receive from God, the *source*. The rain of His word soaks deeply into the soil of your spirit. His Word *energizes* your spirit. As your spirit swells with the life in His Word, your spirit's components begin mixing with this life. The life in His Word prepares your spirit for the *purpose* of God thoughts. The life causes your spirit "to bear" faith *energy* and "to sprout" seed answers, seed provisions, seed directions, and seed instructions. You have faith energy for believing and trusting what you have heard. The faith energy does not stop working in your heart after the first sprouts appear; instead, it continues... faith *continues* through your action upon the God Thought during the ripening period, perhaps working through challenges to your faith, until your harvest time. Faith energy produces the harvest in your heart soil (spirit) before you actually have it in your physical life.

What is happening to the seed thought during the continuation of time? Your seed thought is maturing, and when it is ready, it becomes real in your physical life. This helps our understanding of Hebrews 11:1, which says, "Now faith is the substance of things hoped for, the evidence of things not seen."

What am I specifically referring to as your *physical life*? Your physical life includes all that you are in this world: your spirit, soul (mind, will, and emotions), your body, and the things around you. The physical manifestation of your seed faith occurs when your hope has become sight. The Apostle Paul writes, "But hope that is seen is not hope; for why does one also hope for what he sees?"[2] It is something you can see and feel in your physical life that began with the seed of a God Thought. So, God thoughts must have these four things to cause success in your life: 1) your "hearing ear," 2) your recognition, 3) your acceptance, and 4) your action. When these work together by faith, they bring joy and satisfaction to God because His thought succeeds and accomplishes what He desires in the matter. His will on earth is accomplished, and that brings well-being for you and for others.

REFLECTION

What is the marvelous privilege you possess, being created in God's image and in His likeness?

God understands your learning process. What does He use to help you learn about Him?

What scripture passage is used to describe God's Two-Way Street?

Name the three characteristics of rain and snow. These characteristics work by physical laws that God created. Describe how each one works in the earth, as explained by the author.

What makes the earth "to bear and sprout?"

What is the purpose of rain and snow?

What is the end of the natural cycle for rain and snow?

POWER POINTS

Isaiah 55:10 states that the water "makes the earth to bear and sprout." Have you noticed that the earth is equipped with what it needs for this? The earth is not toiling but allowing the water to mix with it so that it can bring forth life from the seed. Likewise, your heart is not toiling to produce faith for your God thought either. Your heart has every spiritual component it needs to mix with the life energy in God's Word. Jesus' teaching in Mark 4:26-29 tells us that the farmer plants his seed. He goes to bed, gets up, and finds that his crop has come up. He is not bothered about how that happened. He only trusts that it will happen. Jesus said the Kingdom of God is like that. We should not worry but only trust that the Word will produce our crop.

Describe effective communication.

Describe what the author means by the "easy manner" God said His thoughts come?

God is using a natural law to explain a supernatural law. He is saying that His Word accomplishing its purpose follows the same process as that of rain and snow coming to the earth. His word has a source, energy, and a purpose. Briefly describe what each characteristic is doing in the soil of your spirit.

Why does faith energy continue to work after the first sprouts appear?

POWER POINTS

The purposes of rain and snow and His Word are the same: to bring forth life. The water causes the earth to bear and sprout food. Likewise, His Word causes your spirit to bear and sprout answers for your physical life. By faith, your spirit will bring these answers into physical manifestation. The purpose of His Word coming to you is to supply you with God's will in the matter.

"Now faith is the substance of things hoped for; the evidence of things not seen." (Hebrews 11:1)

Physical life refers to what?

When does faith become sight?

Romans 8:24 states what?

List four things that are required for God thoughts to produce success in your life.

When these four work together by faith, why does it bring joy and satisfaction to God?

---

[1] 2 Timothy 3:16
[2] Romans 8:24, 25

CHAPTER 9

GETTING STARTED ON GOD'S "TWO-WAY STREET"

Getting started requires nothing more than writing thoughts under two different headings. The idea is to keep it simple so that you can focus on 1) *My Thoughts to Him,* and 2) *His Thoughts to Me.* It is important to use the headings so that you can easily distinguish between your thoughts and God's thoughts. Take as much space as you need for writing under each heading.

Like no other journal that I have seen, this journal has God's two-way street in mind. You will find that the concept invites expectation of both directions of prayer: the upward and the downward. You will become more aware of God thoughts simply because you create a heading for recording these thoughts.

Dating the entries is optional. Yet, there is something about tracking the time sequence that is valuable for later reflections and comparisons.

When you start your journal, please be at ease. God knows your schedule, and He knows your energy level. God is not challenging you for quantity; He is welcoming you. He has no test that examines how long you must write or how often you must write. You may start with good intentions only to find that they fizzle out. Do not give up! Simply pick up where you left off, and begin resting once again in God's grace. You will find—as I did—your own comfort level of time. It may be every day at the same time and place, and it may be at altogether different times and places.

MY THOUGHTS TO HIM

Jesus said that, from out of the heart, the mouth speaks.[1] Thoughts are expressed from your heart, so express all that is in your heart to God. Express your thoughts to God about your situations, people, worries, inquiries, dreams, longings, confessions of sin, faith confessions, praises, songs, thanksgivings, and so on. Include all of your needs and desires. It is not selfish to express your desires to God. Be honest and forthcoming with all personal thoughts. We make this hard by thinking He won't accept us if we are honest or if He really knew what we were thinking. He already knows, and He first loved you before you ever knew Him.[2] All of your thoughts are safe with Him.

HIS THOUGHTS TO ME

You must be determined to write down every thought you *receive,* whether you think it is a valid God thought or not. Stay focused on Him. Expect His thoughts. This is important. Expect them and record them. These exercises will help you to exercise your "hearing ear." You are training your spiritual ear to hear. Many times, God thoughts come later after you have spent time in your journal. Go record them right away, if possible. If not it is not possible to record them immediately, make some kind of notation so you will not forget the thought.

REFLECTION

What is the purpose of the God Thoughts Journal?

What do you become more aware of with this unique journaling format?

Without these two things, you will not progress very far with God thoughts. Name them and explain what they mean to you.

From where do thoughts proceed, according to Matthew 15:18?

The author instructs you to do what with all of your thoughts?

Are your thoughts safe with God? Why?

---

[1] Matthew 15:18
[2] 1 John 4:19

CHAPTER 10

COMMITTING TO A 40-DAY JOURNAL EXPERIENCE

Fine tuning your spiritual ear to gain knowledge for judgment of God thoughts requires regular journaling. I encourage you to commit to a 40-day journal experience. This is a way for you to get better acquainted with God as your Father and to know what He has planned for you.

I know about busy lives. In one of my busiest seasons ever—working a full-time job, caring for three active sons in high school and college, church activities, teaching Sunday school and weekly Bible studies, and restoring an old house located in another town—I heard God speak this into my thoughts. He said, "If you will come aside to Me for 15 minutes when I call, I will multiply the time as if it were an hour." It was evident to me that God truly desires time with us, even if it is only for 15 minutes.

I have no explanation for how spending time with God multiplies our earthly time, except in this way. I believe God does it the same way He multiplied the two small fish and five loaves of bread that fed over 5,000 people.[1]   Multiplication came by the blessing that Jesus said over the fish and bread.

Every time Jesus blessed something, good things happened. I thought, "Why not follow His example and speak a blessing over my journal time with God?" I suggest praying the blessing found in Numbers 6:24-26 that the high priest, Aaron, said over the people of Israel. Make it personal by inserting yourself in it, and thank the Lord God for multiplying your time with Him.

For a lasting relationship to survive, it must have faithfulness. Keeping faithfulness alive and growing in faithfulness require desire and practice. It is my hope that, after this 40-day experience, you will be thrilled with your increased level of discernment, knowledge, confidence, and results from the actions you took on God thoughts. It is also my hope that a journaling habit becomes an on-going part of your life, one motivated by excitement and expectation of God's next thoughts for you.

THE JOURNAL'S PERSONAL SIDE

In my opinion, we need a renewed focus on the personal side of communication. In some cases, 21st-century technology has caused us to fellowship less, have less face-to-face conversation, and have less friendly warm expressions—all for the sake of convenience.

I am not against technology or convenience, so please do not take me wrong. I am awed by "smart" machines designed for my convenience and have admiration for tech-savvy people who help me operate them. Computers of all descriptions fit well into my life and in yours as useful tools for accomplishing a multitude of purposes. As useful as personal computers can be for holding tons of personal information, they are wholly impersonal, being only a machine.

Is a large portion of your day filled with these machines that cannot transmit personal, warm exchanges? After that kind of day, would you enjoy time with someone who understands you and your needs?

I am thankful that technology has not changed God. He is not and never has been impersonal with His children. He is love, and He loves spending time with you. Everything He did in Christ Jesus was for you, personally. So, instead of reaching for the keyboard of your computer, reach for your pen and this journal. Penning your thoughts on real paper, having something you can feel and hold with your hand, and seeing the data—yours and God's in your own handwriting—all give unspoken comfort to your human senses and energize your mind. The journal needs only your thoughts and God's thoughts, you two in personal conversation.

REAPING RESULTS THAT MATTER

Your fellowship with God, your prayer life, and your walk in obedience with God matter very much to Him. Growing to maturity in the things that matter to God is at the heart of this book. He has provided the material and the opportunities for maturity. You will gain greater and deeper understanding of God as your Father.

As your relationship develops, you will grow in awareness of these things:

1) God loves and cares for you greatly.
2) His greatest pleasure is being with you.
3) Doubt and indecision move out of your way. In their place, comes recognition of every thought received as well as what to do with them.
4) Your hearing ear matures in judgment so that the devil cannot cheat you out God's will for your life.

You need God thoughts for dealing with the pressures of our world. Our world is very different from the perfect one in the Garden with Adam and Eve. God is still doing what He did for them when the world was perfect. He has never stopped being the Father and God, the Provider, the Healer, the Teacher-Counselor, and the Savior. Results that matter for you will happen because you have God thoughts that bring answers: a solution, a plan, a success, an escape, a healing, a repair, a reconciliation, a redeeming peace, a recaptured hope, an abounding grace, an assurance of love, and countless second chances… the list goes on. Your prayer life becomes a living source of strength that produces fearless obedience to God thoughts.

REFLECTION

In view of the communication technologies that have emerged in the 21st century, briefly tell why the author feels there is a need for a return to the more personal side of communication. Mention how the God Thoughts Journal helps you with feeling personally involved with God.

A lasting relationship needs what to survive?

Describe the author's hope for the reader?

"For the word of God is living and active and sharper than any two-edged sword, and piercing as far as the division of soul and spirit, of both joint and marrow, and able to judge the thoughts and intentions of the heart." (Hebrews 4:12)

What matters to God as described in this section?

What result is at the heart of this book?

What four things increase as a result of this book?

Why do you need God thoughts for your life today?

Describe the understanding you gained from the author's story of one of her busiest times.

What benefits are received by speaking a blessing over your time with God?

What causes faithfulness in a relationship to grow?

POWER POINTS

"The LORD bless thee and keep thee. The LORD make his face to shine upon thee, and be gracious unto thee. The LORD lift up his countenance upon thee, and give thee peace." *(Numbers 6:24-26, KJV)*

---

[1] Mark 6:41-43.

CHAPTER 11

MY CONCLUDING THOUGHT

My own journaling style is a good gift to share with you. I believe that it will help you recognize, take ownership for, and act on God thoughts for your life.

The inspiration came from what I was doing in my prayer time with God. I was noting my thoughts, my desires, and what I considered to be God thoughts as answers to them, using scripture references when I needed clarity. I discovered that God answered at times with references in His Word. Other times, He would respond with quick responses. At others, He would give open-ended responses that made me think things through.

Some God thoughts developed into lessons that I taught to others. Writing these thoughts in a journal helped me to organize them topically and made it easier to recall them. My entire journal-writing experience has brought me into God's presence in a way that no other experience has. I have experienced God's presence through worship, prayer, and reading His Word. These are marvelous as well, and I look forward to more. When I journal His thoughts, I allow them to take my focus off my problems and give God my best attention to His plans, which include taking care of me. I feel a part of His team. We work together by exchanging our thoughts.

Let me assure you… God is waiting to meet with you. The journal is in your hands.

"Call unto Me and I will answer you, and show you great and mighty things which you do not know." (Jeremiah 33:3)

THE GOD THOUGHTS JOURNAL

Day 1

MY THOUGHTS (TO GOD)   GOD'S THOUGHTS (TO ME)

DAY 2

MY THOUGHTS (TO GOD)	GOD'S THOUGHTS (TO ME)

DAY 3

MY THOUGHTS (TO GOD)   GOD'S THOUGHTS (TO ME)

_____ | _____
_____ | _____
_____ | _____
_____ | _____
_____ | _____
_____ | _____
_____ | _____
_____ | _____
_____ | _____
_____ | _____
_____ | _____
_____ | _____
_____ | _____
_____ | _____
_____ | _____
_____ | _____
_____ | _____
_____ | _____

Day 4

My Thoughts (to God)	God's Thoughts (to Me)

DAY 5

MY THOUGHTS (TO GOD)	GOD'S THOUGHTS (TO ME)

DAY 6

MY THOUGHTS (TO GOD)	GOD'S THOUGHTS (TO ME)

DAY 7

MY THOUGHTS (TO GOD)   GOD'S THOUGHTS (TO ME)

DAY 8

MY THOUGHTS (TO GOD)	GOD'S THOUGHTS (TO ME)

DAY 9

MY THOUGHTS (TO GOD)	GOD'S THOUGHTS (TO ME)

DAY 10

MY THOUGHTS (TO GOD)	GOD'S THOUGHTS (TO ME)

DAY 11

MY THOUGHTS (TO GOD)   GOD'S THOUGHTS (TO ME)

DAY 12

MY THOUGHTS (TO GOD)   GOD'S THOUGHTS (TO ME)

Day 13

My Thoughts (to God)   God's Thoughts (to Me)

DAY 14

MY THOUGHTS (TO GOD)   GOD'S THOUGHTS (TO ME)

Day 15

My Thoughts (to God)	God's Thoughts (to Me)

DAY 16

MY THOUGHTS (TO GOD)	GOD'S THOUGHTS (TO ME)

DAY 17

MY THOUGHTS (TO GOD)   GOD'S THOUGHTS (TO ME)

DAY 18

MY THOUGHTS (TO GOD)	GOD'S THOUGHTS (TO ME)

DAY 19

MY THOUGHTS (TO GOD)	GOD'S THOUGHTS (TO ME)

DAY 20

MY THOUGHTS (TO GOD)	GOD'S THOUGHTS (TO ME)

DAY 21

MY THOUGHTS (TO GOD)　　　　　GOD'S THOUGHTS (TO ME)

DAY 22

MY THOUGHTS (TO GOD)   GOD'S THOUGHTS (TO ME)

DAY 23

My Thoughts (to God)   God's Thoughts (to Me)

DAY 24

MY THOUGHTS (TO GOD)	GOD'S THOUGHTS (TO ME)

DAY 25

MY THOUGHTS (TO GOD)   GOD'S THOUGHTS (TO ME)

DAY 26

MY THOUGHTS (TO GOD)	GOD'S THOUGHTS (TO ME)

DAY 27

MY THOUGHTS (TO GOD)	GOD'S THOUGHTS (TO ME)

DAY 28

MY THOUGHTS (TO GOD)	GOD'S THOUGHTS (TO ME)

DAY 29

MY THOUGHTS (TO GOD)   GOD'S THOUGHTS (TO ME)

DAY 30

MY THOUGHTS (TO GOD)	GOD'S THOUGHTS (TO ME)

Day 31

My Thoughts (to God)	God's Thoughts (to Me)

DAY 32

MY THOUGHTS (TO GOD)　　　　　GOD'S THOUGHTS (TO ME)

DAY 33

MY THOUGHTS (TO GOD)	GOD'S THOUGHTS (TO ME)

DAY 34

MY THOUGHTS (TO GOD)   GOD'S THOUGHTS (TO ME)

DAY 35

MY THOUGHTS (TO GOD)	GOD'S THOUGHTS (TO ME)

DAY 36

MY THOUGHTS (TO GOD)   GOD'S THOUGHTS (TO ME)

Day 37

My Thoughts (to God)	God's Thoughts (to Me)

DAY 38

MY THOUGHTS (TO GOD)   GOD'S THOUGHTS (TO ME)

DAY 39

MY THOUGHTS (TO GOD)   GOD'S THOUGHTS (TO ME)

DAY 40

MY THOUGHTS (TO GOD)	GOD'S THOUGHTS (TO ME)

BIBLE VERSES FOR JUDGING THOUGHTS

We have the light of His Word as the judge of all our thoughts and actions. His Word is our standard of measure. The following scriptures will help you measure true God thoughts.

"The word of the LORD is right and all his works are done in truth." (Psalms 33:4-11)

"God's wisdom leads to soundness that keeps to the paths of judgment, equity, and every good path... full of discretion... understanding to deliver you from the way of the evil men that walk in the ways of darkness." (Proverbs 1:8-13)

"God's ways are ways of pleasantness." (Proverbs 3:17)

"Thoughts that grant you to be strengthened with might by his Spirit in the inner man." (Ephesians 3:16)

"Thoughts that reflect love, joy, peace, longsuffering, gentleness, goodness, faith, meekness, and temperance." (Galatians 5:22-23)

"Finally, brethren, whatever is true, whatever is honorable, whatever is right, whatever is pure, whatever is lovely, whatever is of good repute, if there is any excellence and if anything worthy of praise, let your mind dwell on these things." (Philippians 4:8)

BIBLE VERSES DESCRIBING GOD'S CHARACTER AND HIS WAYS

"[God's wisdom] speaks of excellent things; and the opening of my lips shall be right things. [God] speaks truth; wickedness is an abomination to his lips... there is nothing froward or perverse in His words... they are all plain to him that understands and right to them find knowledge... prudence prevails. The fear of the LORD is to hate evil: pride and arrogancy and the evil way, and the froward mouth, do I hate. Counsel is mind and sound wisdom." (Proverbs 8:6-12)

"God loves righteousness and judgment." (Psalms 33:4-5)

"The LORD is compassionate and gracious, slow to anger and abounding in lovingkindess." (Psalms 103:8, NASB)

"But God, who is rich in mercy, for his great love wherewith he loved us." (Ephesians 2:4)

"The Lord is full of compassion and tender mercy." (James 5:11)

"God is holy in all manner of conversation." (Leviticus 11:44)

"Be ye holy; for I am holy." (1 Peter 1:15)

"God is not a respecter of persons." (1 Peter 1:17)

"God is light and in him is no darkness at all." (1 John 1:5)

"God loves a cheerful giver." (2 Corinthians 9:7)

"Cast all our cares on him, because He cares for us." (1 Peter 5:7)

"The goodness of God leads to repentance." (Romans 2:4)

"There has no temptation taken you but such as is common to man: but God is faithful, who will not suffer you to be tempted above that ye are able; but will with the temptation also make a way to escape, that you may be able to bear." (1 Corinthians 10:13)

> Nowhere in this scripture does it say that God will not put any more on you than you can bear. God is providing an escape, a way out for you. He is not the one putting any burden, temptation, or trial on you.

"Let no man say when he is tempted, I am tempted of God: for God cannot be tempted with evil, neither tempteth he any man: But every man is tempted, when he is drawn away of his own lust, and enticed." (James 1:13-14, KJV)

> Satan is the tempter and the oppressor. God is the one who delivers you from temptation by providing a way of escape.

"God is Love." (1 John 4:8)

"Love is patient, kind, is not jealous, does not brag and is not arrogant, does act unbecomingly does not seek its own, is not provoked, does not take into account a wrong suffered, does not rejoice in unrighteousness but rejoices with the truth, bears all things, believes all things, hopes all things, endures all things. Love never fails." (1 Corinthians 13:4-8a)